AMAZING HISTORY

SHIPWRECKS

JAMES STEWART

W

FRANKLIN WATTS

An Appleseed Editions book

First published in 2007 by Franklin Watts

Franklin Watts
338 Euston Road, London NW1 3BH

Franklin Watts Australia
Level 17/207 Kent St, Sydney, NSW 2000

© 2007 Appleseed Editions

Appleseed Editions Ltd
Well House, Friars Hill, Guestling, East Sussex TN35 4ET

Created by Q2A Media
Series Editor: Jean Coppendale
Designers: Diksha Khatri, Ashita Murgai
Picture Researchers: Lalit Dalal, Jyoti Sachdev
Illustrators: Hemant Arya, Manish Prasad, Amir Khan

ISBN   978 0 7496 7535 6

Dewey classification: 363.123

All words in **bold** can be found in the glossary on page 30.

Website information is correct at time of going to press. However, the publishers cannot
accept liability for any information or links found on third-party websites.

A CIP catalogue for this book is available from the British Library.

Picture credits
t=top b=bottom c=centre l=left r=right m=middle
Cover images: The Bridgeman Art Library/ Photolibrary: background, Jubal Harshaw/ Shutterstock: b.
Back cover: Q2A Media: tl, tm, tr
Library Of Congress: 4b, 5b, 8b, Oxford Scientific Films/ Photolibrary: 5t, Q2A Media: 6b, 13b, 14, 16,
Bettmann/ Corbis: 7t, 9t, 27b, The British Library Board: 8b, 15t, Jukka Nurminen, Finland: 9b,
VASAMUSEET: 10b, Johan Avard: 11b, Sten Sjostrand/ Nanhai Marine Archaeology Sdn. Bhd.: 12b, 13t, Corbis: 17t,
Photo Researchers, Inc./ Photolibrary: 18b, National Oceanic & Atmospheric Administration (NOAA): 19b, 28b,
ullstein- Willy Stower: 19t, Stuart Williamson 2007: 20b, Navy.mil: 21, 22b, 23t, Michael Pocock: 24b,
Reuters/ Corbis: 25b, Exxon Valdez Oil Spill Trustee Council: 26t, 26b, Daniel Gustavsson/ Shutterstock: 29.

Printed in China

Franklin Watts is a division of Hachette Children's Books

Contents

Why do ships sink?

When the sea rages, ships can be seriously damaged or wrecked. But shipwrecks can be caused by many other things, such as an explosion on board or a sudden leak, a **collision** or **running aground**, a fire or error of **navigation**.

Explosion

On 15 February 1898, the US **battleship** *Maine* was tied up in Havana **harbour**, Cuba, when suddenly it exploded. This shipwreck helped to spark a war between Spain and America. Later, the ship's own **gunpowder** was found to have exploded by accident.

HOTSPOTS

In 2002, two cargo ships, the Tricolour and the Kariba, collided in the English Channel. The Tricolour sank with 2,862 luxury cars on board.

The explosion of the US battleship *Maine*, which killed 260 men.

The wreckage of the Chinese gunboat *Tien Sing*, on St John's Reef, in the Red Sea. A navigation error led to the ship's bottom being ripped out on the dangerous reef.

On the rocks

The SS *Princess May* hit a **reef** close to Alaska's Sentinel Island on 5 August 1910, in full view of the **lighthouse**. As the tide went out, the ship stayed perched dangerously on the jagged rocks. All 80 passengers and 68 **crew** were rescued.

The *Princess May* was trapped on the rocks for almost a month. The ship was pulled free by tug boats.

Up in the air!
People waiting to be rescued

The Mary Rose

Shipwrecks do not always happen in storms. Sometimes sailors or shipbuilders make a mistake and a ship sinks in calm weather. This is what happened to the *Mary Rose*.

Pride of a king

The *Mary Rose* was Henry VIII's favourite and finest warship. In 1545, after many battles and having been fitted with powerful new guns, it sailed out from Portsmouth Harbour to attack the French **fleet**. But before firing a single shot, the ship turned – and sank! The sea had flooded in through the open gun ports, making the ship top-heavy.

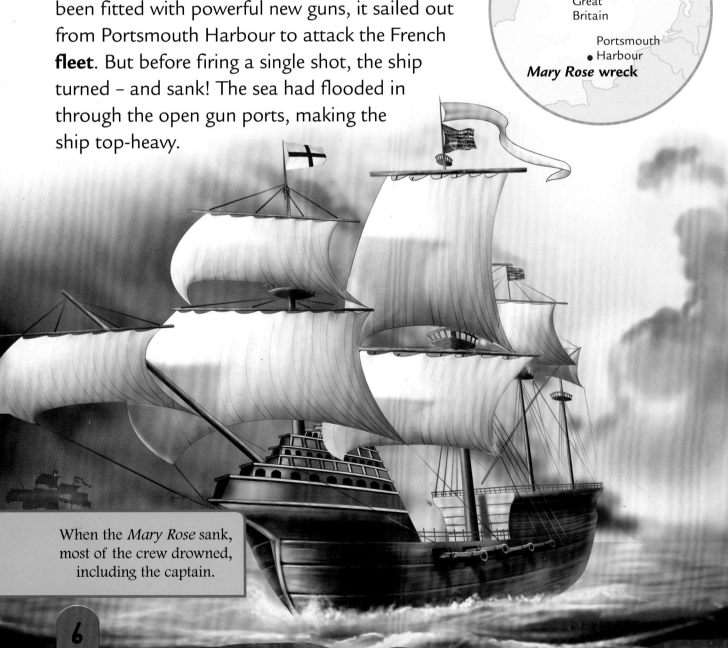

Great Britain

Portsmouth
Harbour
Mary Rose wreck

When the *Mary Rose* sank, most of the crew drowned, including the captain.

BABCOCK POWER CONSTRUCTION DIVISION

T.C.W.I   WULF CUXHAVEN

Up, up and away
A lifting frame was used to raise the wreck

Strong support
A support cradle protected the fragile wooden remains

The wreck of the *Mary Rose* was finally rescued in 1982. It is now restored and on display in Portsmouth.

Raising the wreck

The *Mary Rose* lay on the seabed for 437 years. It was lifted on 11 October 1982, and work to restore it began in 1994. In 2003–4, parts of the ship's left side were found at the bottom of the sea. These large pieces of wood had probably broken away from the ship when it sank. Over 22,000 valuable items were found on the wreck, including navigation equipment, guns and board games.

HOTSPOTS
Built between 1509 and 1511, the Mary Rose was named after King Henry VIII's favourite sister, Mary. The rose was the **Tudor** *family emblem.*

Treasure ships

When Spain ruled large parts of the **New World**, it used **galleons** to carry treasure, such as gold and silver, across the Atlantic to Europe. But these treasure ships attracted pirates, and their battles led to many shipwrecks.

Pirates and privateers

Pirates were often hired by their home country to rob enemy ships of their treasure. Many pirates, or **privateers** as they were known, came from France and England. One of the most famous was Francis Drake. In 1587, Drake turned from piracy to warfare. He led an English fleet into the Spanish harbour of Cadiz, and set fire to many enemy ships.

Francis Drake attacking a Spanish treasure ship.

HOTSPOTS

After sailing around the world in his ship, the Golden Hind, *Francis Drake was knighted by Queen Elizabeth 1 in 1581.*

The sinking of the SS Golden Gate

On 27 July 1862, the *SS Golden Gate* left San Francisco and headed for Panama. On board were 338 passengers and crew, plus $1,400,000 in gold. Tragically, the voyage was never completed. The steamship caught fire and sank off the coast of Manzanillo, Mexico, and more than 200 people died.

Only 100 passengers survived the wreck of the *Golden Gate*.

On the rocks

The ship was driven on to rocks, which smashed its **rudder**

The wreck of the *Vrouw Maria* (Virgin Mary), which sank during a storm in 1771, off the coast of Finland. The wooden merchant ship was sailing to St Petersburg in Russia.

The Vasa

In 1626, King Gustavus Adolphus of Sweden ordered a huge warship to be built. Named after his royal house, *Vasa*, he wanted the ship for the war against his neighbour, Poland.

Harbour disaster

At the time, the *Vasa* was the greatest ship ever built. The **hull** was five metres tall and carried 64 heavy, **brass cannons**. The *Vasa* set sail for the first time on 10 August 1628. As it sailed out of Stockholm Harbour, crowds cheered and the ship fired its guns to celebrate. Suddenly, a gust of wind caught the sails. The ship lurched, leaned heavily to one side and stayed there. Ten minutes after leaving port, the *Vasa* sank.

Sweden

Stockholm

Poland

As the *Vasa* started to lean over, sea water flooded in through the open gun ports.

Decked out
The *Vasa* had two gun decks instead of one, which made it extra heavy

Great escape
Most of the crew escaped from the sinking *Vasa*

Raising the Vasa

The wreck of the *Vasa* was still in good condition when it was found. Attempts to raise it began in 1956 and took five years to complete. After drilling tunnels beneath its **keel**, cables were passed through these tunnels and the ship was lifted to the surface. While it was still under water, divers repaired the wreck with oak pegs and wooden padded covers. The *Vasa* finally appeared above the water on 24 April 1961.

HOTSPOTS

Many fascinating treasures were found in the wreck of the Vasa, including the officers' pewter dinner service, bronze candlesticks, barrels of meat, a coat of arms and silver and bronze coins from the 17th century.

The *Vasa* has now been restored and is on display in a specially built museum in Skansen, in Sweden.

Golden carvings

The wooden carvings were painted gold. They showed emperors, knights, lions, monsters and mermaids

Chinese treasure wrecks

During the 15th century, the Chinese travelled great distances in huge ships with cargoes of valuable pottery and silk. Some of these ships were wrecked. They are still being discovered and their treasures sold to collectors around the world.

The Royal Nanhai

In 1994, the wreck of a Chinese junk, the *Royal Nanhai*, was found in the South China Sea, off the coast of Malaysia. Archaeologists think this huge ship broke up in heavy seas around 1460. It was probably taking a **cargo** of valuable **porcelain** from China to Java. About 20 per cent of this cargo has been recovered in excellent condition and the most valuable pieces are now in museums around the world.

China

India

South China Sea

Malaysia

Royal Nanhai **wreck**

A sketch of the wreck of the *Royal Nanhai* showing porcelain stored below deck.

Precious cargo
Nearly 21,000 pieces of pottery have been recovered

12

A marine archaeologist cleaning some of the precious porcelain found in the wreck of the *Royal Nanhai*.

HOTSPOTS

Admiral Zheng He was given gifts by the rulers of the many countries he visited. He took back the first zebra, giraffe, ostrich and oryx to be seen in China.

Early wrecks

Between 1404 and 1433 the government in China organized seven naval expeditions under the command of Admiral Zeng He. On his first voyage he had 317 ships with over 27,000 crew. These ships were the largest vessels afloat at the time. The fleets sailed to India, the Persian Gulf and down the coast of East Africa. Some were wrecked in storms and lie at the bottom of the ocean.

Christopher Columbus's ship, the *Pinta*, is tiny beside one of Zheng He's ships, which were up to 146 metres long.

Vast masts

Each treasure ship had nine huge masts

A light in the dark

Lighthouses are built by the sea to mark the coastline in the dark. The first lighthouse, built in 290 BC, was in Alexandria, Egypt.

Longstone lighthouse

Great Britain

Eddystone lighthouse

Lights out

In 1703, Henry Winstanley built one of Britain's first lighthouses on the Eddystone Rocks outside Plymouth. He said his wooden building could survive the roughest weather. He was in it when a test came on 26 November 1703. That night, the worst storm ever known hit Britain. The next morning, people went to see if the lighthouse was still there. Horrified, they saw that Winstanley and his building had completely disappeared.

No one can be really sure, but strong winds and the pounding sea probably smashed the Eddystone lighthouse to pieces.

Grace Darling and her father rescued the survivors from a ship wrecked during the night.

All at sea
Grace Darling with her father and other rescuers at sea

Darling rescue

Grace Darling lived with her father in the Longstone lighthouse, on sharp rocks off the coast of Northumberland. One September morning in 1838, the Darlings rowed through rough seas to rescue nine people clinging to rocks. Grace became a heroine and a museum was named after her. Grace and her father were also awarded the Royal National Lifeboat Institution's Silver Medal.

HOTSPOTS

Today, lighthouses are automatic, so people no longer need to live in them. Floating **buoys** with automatic lights or bells also warn sailors of dangerous coasts.

Wreckers!

Rocky coasts are battered by mighty storms that often leave ships torn apart on the rocks. In the past, people living nearby have realized that they could profit from these wrecks... and, some say, not all these shipwrecks were accidents...

Great
Britain

**North
Cornwall**

Free for all

In the dark, captains steered their ships guided by lights on the shore. But what if someone moved a light? It is said **wreckers** did this to lead ships towards rocks, so they could steal the cargo. We do not know why the cargo ship, *Postillion* ran into the coast of north Cornwall in 1732. But we do know that wreckers quickly stripped the vessel of everything valuable that could be carried away.

Wreckers may have waved fire torches to lead ships to smash against dangerous rocks.

Wreckers taking the cargo of brandy from the grounded *Rosina*, off Long Island, New York in 1871. News of a shipwreck spread quickly among local communities, bringing wreckers to the scene to strip the ship of all its cargo.

The wrecking reef

The **looting** of shipwrecks was a very profitable business around the world. In the USA, it was a major industry from the time of the Spanish treasure ships in the 16th century to about 1900. Many ships were grounded on the dangerous reefs around Key West, a small island in the Florida Keys, allowing the locals to loot their cargo.

HOTSPOTS

In the mid-19th century, Key West was one of the richest cities in the USA. Its wealth was mainly due to the wreckers. Many ships sank in the dangerous Gulf area around the Keys. But wreckers were required to save passengers, before looting the ships.

RMS Titanic

The most famous shipwreck of all time took place in 1912. The *Titanic*, weighing 44,000 tonnes, was the largest ship in the world. It was on its first-ever voyage, steaming across the Atlantic Ocean from Southampton to New York.

Unsinkable

The builders of the *Titanic* said their ship was so big and well made that it was 'unsinkable'. How wrong they were! The night of 14 April was calm and clear. The sea was flat and bright stars twinkled in the cold, clear sky. Most of the 2,200 people on board were having a wonderful time.

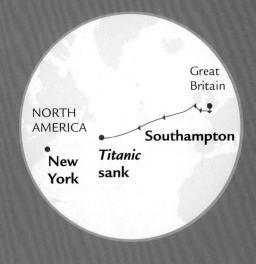

Great Britain

NORTH AMERICA

Southampton

New York

Titanic sank

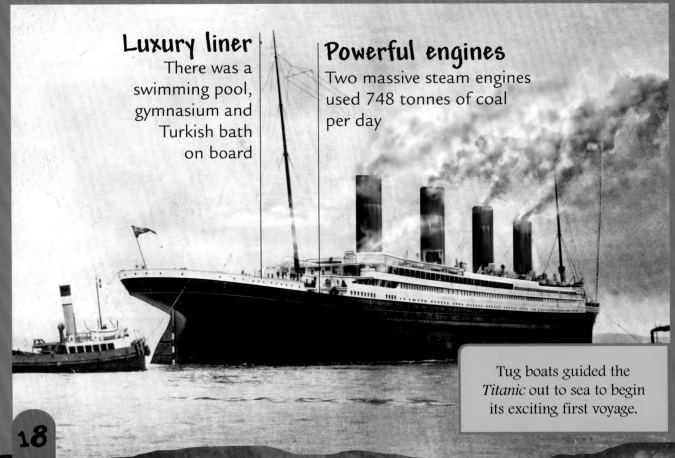

Luxury liner
There was a swimming pool, gymnasium and Turkish bath on board

Powerful engines
Two massive steam engines used 748 tonnes of coal per day

Tug boats guided the *Titanic* out to sea to begin its exciting first voyage.

Icy death

Travelling fast in the dark, the *Titanic* suddenly ran into an iceberg. Water poured in through holes ripped in the side. Slowly, over the next two and a half hours, the ship sank into the freezing Atlantic. There were not enough lifeboats for everyone on board, so 1,500 people drowned. Another ship, the *Californian*, was nearby and could have rescued many, but it thought the *Titanic's* signals for help were fun fireworks!

The law required the *Titanic* to carry only enough lifeboats for half the passengers and crew on board.

HOTSPOTS

Although six iceberg warnings were given on the day the Titanic *sank, the captain believed there was no need to slow down.*

The wreck of the *Titanic* on the ocean floor. It is covered in barnacles and rust.

Wartime shipwrecks

The two world wars were fought as much at sea as on land. Thousands of warships and merchant vessels were wrecked – and tens of thousands of people drowned.

The Lusitania

The most famous shipwreck of World War I was probably the SS *Lusitania*, a passenger ship on the way from the USA to Britain. On 7 May 1915, a German submarine torpedoed the ship to prevent it from taking supplies to Britain. The huge ship sank in just 18 minutes, drowning 1,198 people.

Secret cargo
The *Lusitania* may have carried a secret cargo of weapons and explosives

The *Lusitania* was hit by a torpedo which set off a secondary explosion. The USA was very angry at the number of Americans killed in the disaster. Two years later the USA joined the war against Germany.

Pearl Harbor

On 7 December 1941, Japanese warplanes attacked **Pearl Harbor**, where much of the US Pacific fleet was based. The attack destroyed eight American battleships and 188 planes, severely damaged nine other warships and killed 2,403 American servicemen and 68 **civilians**.

The wrecked destroyers USS *Downes* and USS *Cassin* at the navy yard at Pearl Harbor shortly after the Japanese attack.

Fire!

Ships catch fire for all sorts of reasons, such as electrical faults on board or an enemy attack. Fire was a major hazard aboard wooden ships. Modern ships carry materials, such as paint and fuel, which also burn easily.

Steam pioneer

USS *Missouri* was the first American warship to cross the Atlantic under steam power, arriving in Gibraltar on 25 August 1843. The following evening, an officer accidentally broke a bottle of turpentine in the storeroom, which quickly caught fire. The flames spread so fast, that in four hours the warship became a blackened, sinking wreck.

Rescue
The British ship *Malabar* rescued around 200 of the *Missouri*'s crew

The crew of the *Missouri* barely escaped with their lives.

Up in flames

Northern supply ships were fired on from the city of Vicksburg

The supply ship, *Henry Clay*, caught fire and sank during the bombardment of Vicksburg, Mississippi, by Northern forces in 1863, in the American Civil War.

Guns blazing

Many fierce naval battles were fought during the **American Civil War** between the Northern and Southern States. In 1863, a fleet carrying arms and supplies to the Northern army in the city of Vicksburg, sailed up the Mississippi. Southern forces lit enormous fires along the coast which made the ships easy targets. Remarkably, only one ship, the *Henry Clay*, was destroyed by fire. The other ships landed successfully further down the river and delivered their supplies.

HOTSPOTS

On 9 February 1942, the luxurious ocean liner Normandie, was being refitted to carry soldiers. A spark fell on a pile of life jackets, which quickly caught fire. Fire-fighters poured so much water on the burning ship that it sank!

Harbour disasters

Some of the most serious shipwrecks have happened in the safety of harbours. Just when everyone thought nothing could go wrong, something terrible happened.

Roll over

In 1915, the **liner** *Eastland* was hired to take passengers on a picnic on Lake Michigan. The ship had recently been fitted with bigger lifeboats. By 7am, 2,500 passengers were on board on the river front in Chicago. The weight of the people and the new lifeboats made the *Eastland* top-heavy. The ship suddenly rolled over and more than 800 people were drowned. The water was flat, calm and only six metres deep.

NORTH AMERICA

Lake Michigan

Chicago●

Desperate escape
People can be seen trying to get off the ship. But many people died, trapped below deck

Just as the *Eastland* was about to leave, hundreds of passengers rushed to one side of the deck to get a view of the river – and the ship capsized.

Tragic mistake

On 6 March 1987, the *Herald of Free Enterprise* **ferry** steamed out of Zeebrugge Harbour, Belgium. The ship had big bow doors to allow cars to drive on and off. These doors were left open and, as the ferry picked up speed, the sea poured in. After only 90 seconds the vessel filled with water and turned over on its side. Of the 539 passengers and crew on board, 193 drowned in the United Kingdom's worst peace-time marine tragedy since the sinking of the *Titanic* in 1912.

HOTSPOTS

Ferry disasters are still happening. In 2006, more than 1,000 people died when the Egyptian ferry al-Salam Boccaccio 98 caught fire and sank in the Red Sea.

The *Herald of Free Enterprise* lay on its side as rescue ships took survivors to safety.

Trapped below

Many passengers were eating in the ship's restaurant when the accident happened

Open doors

The ship's doors should have been closed

Polluting wrecks

Modern shipwrecks brought a new peril – **pollution**! During the 20th century, bigger and bigger **tankers** were built to carry oil. When they sank, the oil polluted the sea and shore for kilometres.

Alaska
NORTH AMERICA
Exxon Valdez wreck

Huge disaster

The *Exxon Valdez* was enormous: 300 metres long, 50 metres wide and 27 metres tall. On the night of 24 March 1989, the ship hit a reef off the coast of Alaska and millions of litres of oil poured into the sea.

In 2004, a federal judge ordered Exxon to pay $4.5 billion in damages for the *Valdez* oil spill.

The *Exxon Valdez* oil spill caused the worst-ever sea pollution, killing about 250,000 sea birds, 2,800 sea otters and 300 seals.

Area of oil spill
Stretched for over 750 km

Amount leaked
Enough oil to fill 125 Olympic-sized swimming pools

Bad plans

In 1967, due to a navigation error, the **supertanker** *Torrey Canyon* struck a reef off the coast of Cornwall. British planes tried bombing the tanker to make it sink before its oil leaked into the sea, but this plan did not work. Neither did another to burn the ship's leaking oil. The pollution killed sea life and ruined beaches for hundreds of kilometres around.

Great Britain

Torrey Canyon oil spill •

HOTSPOTS

In 2002, the Prestige *oil tanker was wrecked off the Spanish coast. A year later, its oil was still polluting beaches hundreds of kilometres away.*

Crude oil

The *Torrey Canyon* was one of the world's first supertankers. It carried 120,000 tonnes of oil

This official picture, taken by the Royal Navy on 3 March 1967, shows the stern of the broken *Torrey Canyon* after it had struck Seven Stones Reef off Land's End.

Sea-slick

Leaking oil quickly spread along the Cornish and French coasts

Finding wrecks today

Throughout history, divers have tried to find wrecks and salvage treasure. Modern technology has made this work easier and less dangerous.

The submersible

One of the earliest uses of submarines was to find shipwrecks and salvage treasure. **Submersibles** and **bathyspheres** were among the early submarine models used for this purpose. Modern salvage ships are often semi-submersible, which means that a large part of the vessel is under water. They carry huge electric cranes to lift wrecks when they find them.

Going down

Strong lights are essential in deep water, where it is very dark and murky

The *Johnson Sea-link's* submersible was built in 1971 for deep-sea scientific research.

HOTSPOTS

After a collision on 24 January 1909, the RMS Republic *was wrecked off the coast of Nantucket, USA. Most of the passengers were rescued, but the gold it was carrying for the Tsar of Russia, sank to the bottom of the sea. There have been many attempts to find the treasure, but without success.*

Rescued treasure

We explore wrecks not just for the value of their cargo. Ancient wrecks are like time capsules, which give valuable clues about how people lived in the past. Underwater archaeologists uncover history's secrets by studying their finds in great detail. Divers also explore wrecks for fun. But diving to some wrecks is not allowed as they are of great historic importance or they are war graves.

Take a dive
Divers can spend months and sometimes years searching for a hidden wreck

Many divers risk their lives searching for long-lost ships, in the hope they will learn more about the ship, and how and why it sank.

Glossary

American Civil War (1861–1865) The war fought between the Northern and Southern states of America.

bathysphere A strong, deep-sea diving vehicle, which is lowered by a cable.

battleship A heavily armoured warship, of the late 19th and early 20th centuries.

brass Metal made by mixing copper and tin.

buoy A floating bell or light that warns ships of danger.

cannons Large, heavy guns mounted on wheels, usually fired from a warship.

cargo Goods carried by a ship.

civilians People not in the armed services or police force.

collision When two or more ships crash into each other.

crew People who operate a ship.

ferry Short-distance passenger ship.

fleet A group of ships sailing together under one commander.

galleon A large three-masted sailing ship of the 15th–17th centuries.

gunpowder An explosive made by mixing powdered saltpetre, sulphur and charcoal.

harbour A sheltered port where ships are protected from bad weather.

hull The main body of a ship.

keel The main, long timber or steel support along the base of a ship.

lighthouse A tower on the shore with a light at the top to warn ships.

liner A large passenger ship, one of a group of similar ships owned by the same company or 'line'.

navigation Working out a position, and planning and following a route at sea.

New World A term used to describe North and South America. Also known as the Americas.

Pearl Harbor
A harbour on the island of O'ahu, Hawaii, west of Honolulu in the Pacific Ocean.

pollution The effect of poisonous or harmful substances on the environment or atmosphere.

porcelain Fine, hard chinaware. The process of making porcelain was invented by the Chinese.

privateer A private individual who holds an official government licence to capture enemy merchant shipping.

reef Dangerous ridges of rock, sand or coral in the sea, on which ships are often wrecked.

rudder A device at the rear of a ship used for steering.

run aground When a ship is stranded on the seabed because the water is too shallow.

salvage To save ships or their cargo from destruction or loss at sea.

submersible A small submarine which works under water for short periods. It is designed to operate in deep water, below levels at which divers can work.

supertanker A very large tanker.

tanker A ship that carries liquids, such as oil.

Tudor Kings and queens from the same family who held the English throne from 1485 until 1603.

wreckers Thieves who stole the cargo of wrecked ships.

Index

Webfinder

www.eastlanddisaster.org/summary.htm – Find out more about how a fun day out turned into a tragedy.

www.pirates-shipwrecks-treasure-diving.com/ – All you need to know about hunting for shipwrecks.

www.en.wikipedia.org/wiki/Exxon_valdez_oil_spill – The full story of the *Exxon Valdez* disaster with lots of other links.

www.maryrose.org/ – Take a tour of the Mary Rose Museum, explore the *Mary Rose* and meet the crew.

www.lusitania.net/disaster.htm – A detailed breakdown of the *Lusitania* disaster, the rescue of survivors and the recovery of bodies.